15.50 n.d.
W9-CDS-346

LET'S VISIT

A Printing Plant

by Catherine O'Neill

photography by James W. Parker

Troll Associates

Library of Congress Cataloging in Publication Data

O'Neill, Catherine, (date)
Let's visit a printing plant.

Summary: Follows the processes in a printing plant which produce the books we find in stores, libraries, and schools.
1. Printing, Practical—Juvenile literature.
2. Printing industry—Juvenile literature. 3. Book industries and trade—Juvenile literature. 4. Books—Format—Juvenile literature. [1. Printing, Practical. 2. Book industries and trade] I. Parker, James W., ill. II. Title.
Z244.058 1988 686.2 87-3484
ISBN 0-8167-1163-1 (lib. bdg.)
ISBN 0-8167-1164-X (pbk.)

Printed in the United States of America.
10 9 8 7 6 5 4 3 2 1

The author and publisher wish to thank Marlin Harker and R.R. Donnelley & Sons Company for their generous assistance and cooperation.

There are so many wonderful books to read. It's hard to know which to choose first. It's fun to read about prehistoric times when dinosaurs roamed the earth. Or, take a giant step into the future and read about travel through space. How are books made? Let's visit a printing plant and "read all about it."

Hundreds of thousands of books are made in a printing plant each year. The building holds modern machinery for printing books and putting them together. Cookbooks and math books, nature books and novels—all kinds of books for children and adults are made in a printing plant.

Let's go inside and meet some of the people who help to make it all happen. A worker uses a computer to keep track of the books to be printed at the plant. He sets up schedules for the different projects so that everything will run smoothly.

The first step in preparing a book for printing is *proofreading* all of the pages. The proofreader checks the type for mistakes. It's her last chance to change any words. Another worker uses a machine to mark the margins on a page. The marks will be used as guides so the type on the page will not be crooked.

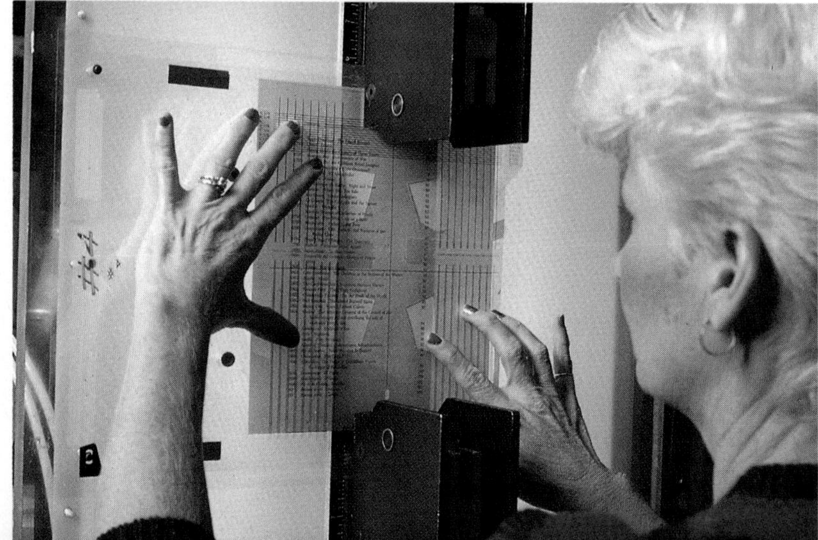

A photographer then makes negative images of the pages of type. These are called *film flats.* A flat is just like the negative of a picture you'd take with your camera. The pictures and words on a flat appear backwards. But when printed they are as they should be.

Holes or scratches on the dark part of a flat become specks on a printed page. A worker must cover them with a special black ink so the camera light can't get through. This is called *opaquing*.

Sample pages, or *blueprints* of the book, are then made from the flats. A piece of equipment, like a copying machine, makes the large paper sheets of words. Printers check the blueprints for any mistakes or problems with the type.

The publishing company that hired the printer also checks the blueprints. An *editor* marks errors that the printer must fix before the book goes to press. Red circles show where type is broken or where a word is misspelled.

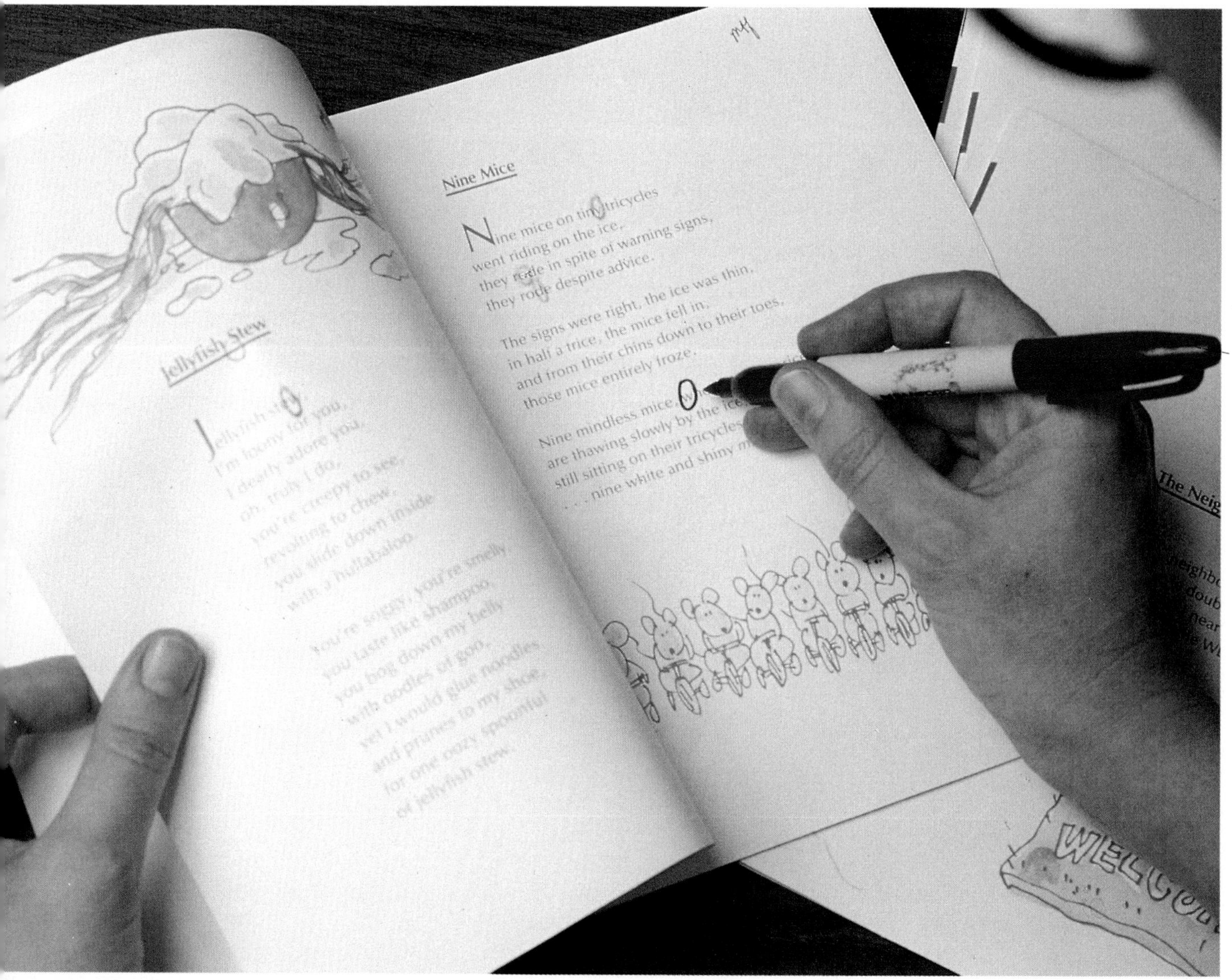

Once all the errors have been corrected, a *printing plate* is made. A blank sheet of aluminum is fed into the machine. Then, out comes a printing plate! Words have been transferred from the flats onto the printing plates.

The aluminum plates are then rolled around cylinders in the printing press. Here, words are printed onto paper—the most important step in making a book! Once the right number of pages have been printed, the plates are destroyed. The film flats are stored. They can be used again to print more copies if a book becomes popular.

It takes a lot of paper to print books. Each of these rolls contains enough paper to print five hundred to a thousand books. The enormous rolls are stored in a warehouse at the printing plant. *Fork lifts* are used to move the rolls from the warehouse to the press room.

Inside the press, words are transferred from the aluminum plates onto paper. How does this happen? In a few simple steps! First, ink is spread onto the printing plates. The plates then roll across a bed of soft rubber called a *blanket.* They deposit ink images of the words onto the blanket. Next, the paper rolls over the blanket and picks up the images, or words.

Paper zooms through the press while being printed. Then it is cut and folded. Mechanical arms fold the sheets into 32-page *signatures*. The machine is designed so that pages are folded in just the right order for reading.

A worker stacks signatures into bundles to be sent to the bindery. Most books have more than one signature, so several must be combined. The first signature contains pages 1 to 32; the second, 33 to 64.

On the *bindery production line,* covers are attached to the pages of the books. Many books have covers made from cloth glued onto cardboard. These are called *hardback books*. *Paperback books* have soft covers made from heavy paper.

Signatures wait until the *gathering machine* is finally set into motion. Then, the signatures drop onto a moving platform called a *conveyor belt.* As the belt moves along, signatures are added to the original set. One or more sets of signatures will form the complete set of pages.

The signatures have been gathered in the right order to make a finished book. Now the gathered pages are turned onto their sides by a set of mechanical arms. They roll under a glue pot which spreads warm glue along the *spine,* or back of the book. Blank sheets of paper called end paper are then added to the pages. Together the pages and end paper form what is known as a *book block.*

Rollers carry the book blocks along. It's almost time to add covers. At another station along the bindery line, glue pellets are melted in a heater. The sticky substance will then be used to attach covers to the book blocks.

A long line of hardback covers moves slowly along a conveyor belt. The book's title, author, and publisher are stamped in gold letters on the spine. At the end of the belt, the covers will move on and be folded over the book blocks.

Pages and cover meet as the book is finally "cased in." The cover is wrapped around the book block. Then it is tightly squeezed. Heat and pressure attach the pages firmly to their case. A metal arm then flips the book into position for the next step—putting on the book jacket.

Book jackets are loose paper covers that protect the hard covers of books. These colorful jackets are made on a machine called a *sheet-fed press*. The sheet-fed press also makes color covers for paperback books. The machine prints words and color pictures onto individual sheets of paper.

Printers keep a watchful eye on the ink in a sheet-fed press. An operator controls the ink flow by adjusting keys on a machine. If the ink is too thick, the colors will be too dark on the finished product. A full-color cover is printed using only four colors: yellow, blue (cyan), red (magenta), and black. When the four colors are mixed together, they combine to make many more colors.

For a cover with many colors, the sheets must be run through four different parts of the press. First, they are run through the part of the press that holds the yellow ink; next, the red; then, the blue; and, finally, the black. At last, all the colors have been combined to make up the cover art!

A supervisor watches as a paperback cover is printed. He wants to be sure that everything is moving along as it should. Another printer uses a *densitometer* to see if the colors have been printed evenly.

After the covers have been printed and dried, they are run through a *laminator.* The machine applies a shiny plastic coating to protect the paper sheets.

At last, the book jackets for some hardback books are about to be placed on each one. The jackets are wrapped around wide-open books. Then the books with their jackets are closed. They move along the conveyor belt on the last stage of their trip.

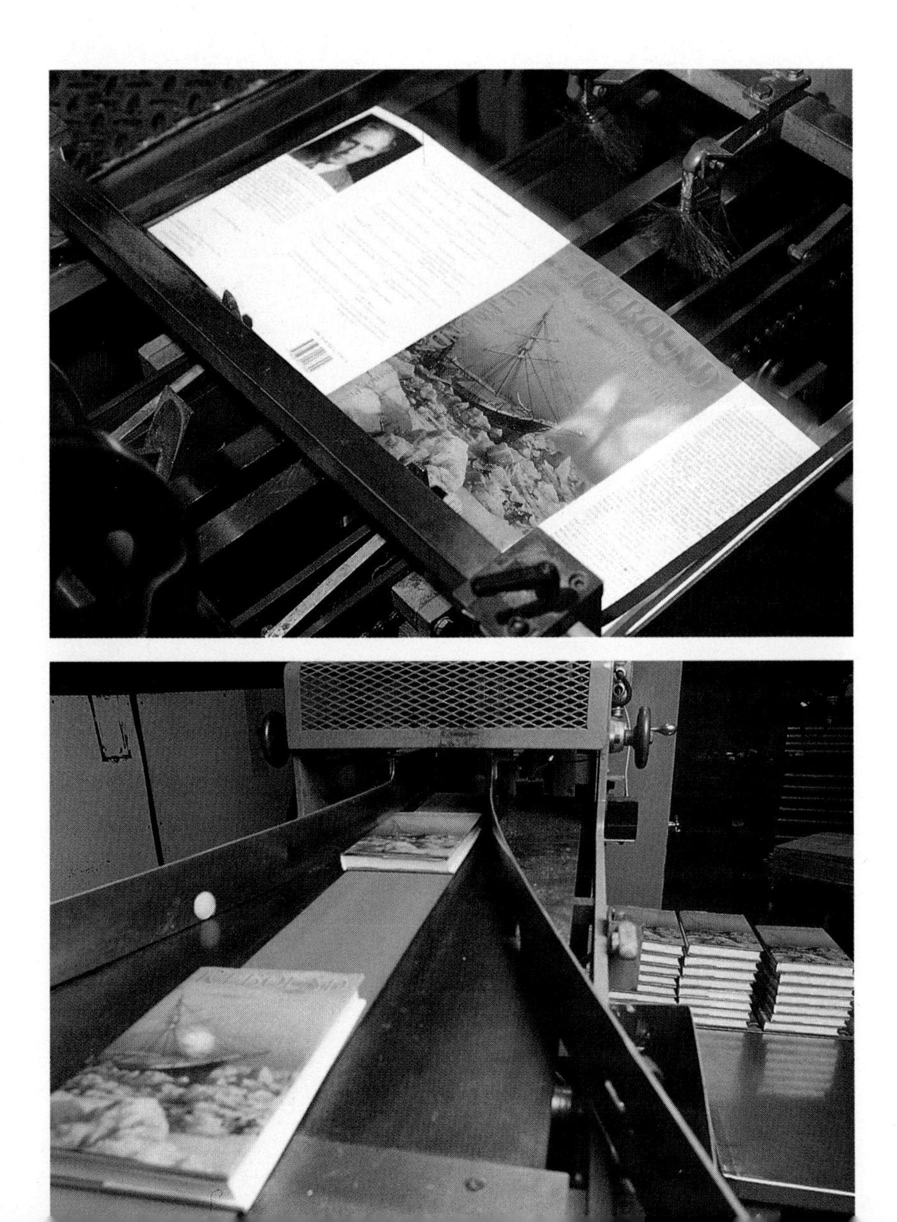

At the end of the bindery production line, a machine stacks all the books. A worker places them in cartons. They are ready to go to the warehouse!

Printed paper that has not been used is *recycled* for later use. First, it is shredded into tiny bits and pressed together into big bundles. Then, the bundles are delivered to paper manufacturers to be made into paper again.

The new books don't stay in the warehouse for long. People are eager to read them. Soon it's time to carry a load of cartons to the loading docks. From there, they'll be shipped to bookstores, libraries, and schools.

A lot of hard work went into making each book on your library shelf. Books can be fun, exciting, informative. Have *you* read a good book lately?